Small's Big Journey

A True Story of Freedom and the Fight for the Vote

by
Charlene Butts Ligon

ISBN 978-0-9993836-3-6 — Paperback
ISBN 978-0-9993836-5-0 — Hardcover
ISBN 978-0-9993836-4-3 — Ebook

Published by
Smallwood Charlotte Press
Carrollton, Virginia, USA

Printed in the United States of America

This book is based on historical records and family history preserved by descendants of Smallwood Ackiss.

Author/Art Direction by Charlene Butts Ligon
Art refinement and illustration support by Ahmed Raafat Abbas

Library of Congress Cataloging-in-Publication data available upon request.

First edition, 2026

Smallwood Ackiss was born long ago in Virginia Beach. He lived near the water at Birdneck Point, by Linkhorn Bay. His family called him Small.

Tall trees grew across the land.
Wide fields reached toward the water.
The water shimmered far away.

But Small was born into slavery. He had no say in where he lived, what he learned, or how he spent his days.

When he was a boy, he held a quiet dream in his heart, a dream of freedom.

But for Small, it was also a place of hard work, where he waited and hoped for the day freedom would come.

Small worked in the fields from sunup to sundown. He chopped wood, carried water, and looked after animals. Still, deep inside, he knew he was meant for more.

Deep inside, he held on to hope.

In those days, slave owners controlled the churches.
Black families could come, but they had to sit in the back.

Still, the church gave Smallwood strength.
People prayed together. Voices rose.

Small and Charlotte stood with other families.
They held on to hope.

They believed freedom would come.
They believed tomorrow would be better.

When the service ended, families stepped outside into the warm afternoon light.

They walked slowly down a dusty road.
They spoke in quiet voices.
They talked about what they heard and what they hoped for.

Some spoke of learning to read.
Some spoke of freedom.
Some spoke of what the future might bring.

As they made their way home, Small grew quiet.
That night, he whispered,
“Lord, help me stand tall.”

As time passed, the world around Small began to change. The Civil War had begun, and word spread that Black men were joining the Union Army.

Small listened closely. He knew freedom was not simply given. It had to be fought for.

When the time came, Small stepped forward. He became a soldier in the United States Colored Troops, Company E, 23rd Regiment.

Small was now a soldier in the Union Army, ready to stand for freedom.

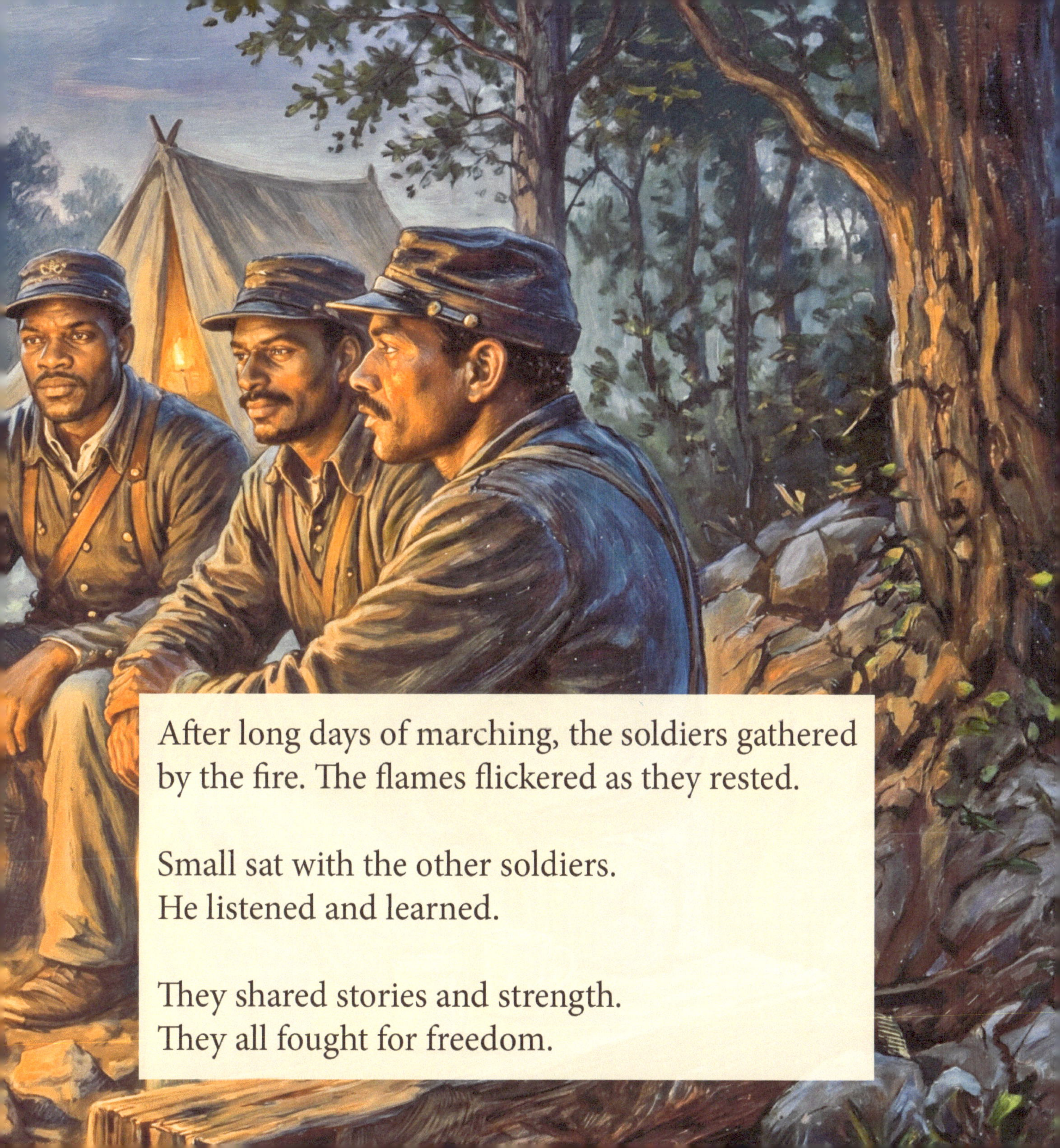

After long days of marching, the soldiers gathered by the fire. The flames flickered as they rested.

Small sat with the other soldiers.
He listened and learned.

They shared stories and strength.
They all fought for freedom.

When the war ended, Small and Charlotte built a cabin. They grew crops and raised their family.

Small was given 30 acres of land. It was land where he had once been enslaved.

From the soil, new life rose.

Small and Charlotte raised their children with love and purpose.

In their home, freedom was more than a word. It was the life they were building together.

Freedom meant more than leaving the fields. It meant being heard.

Small walked toward town, steady and unafraid. For the first time, his voice would matter.

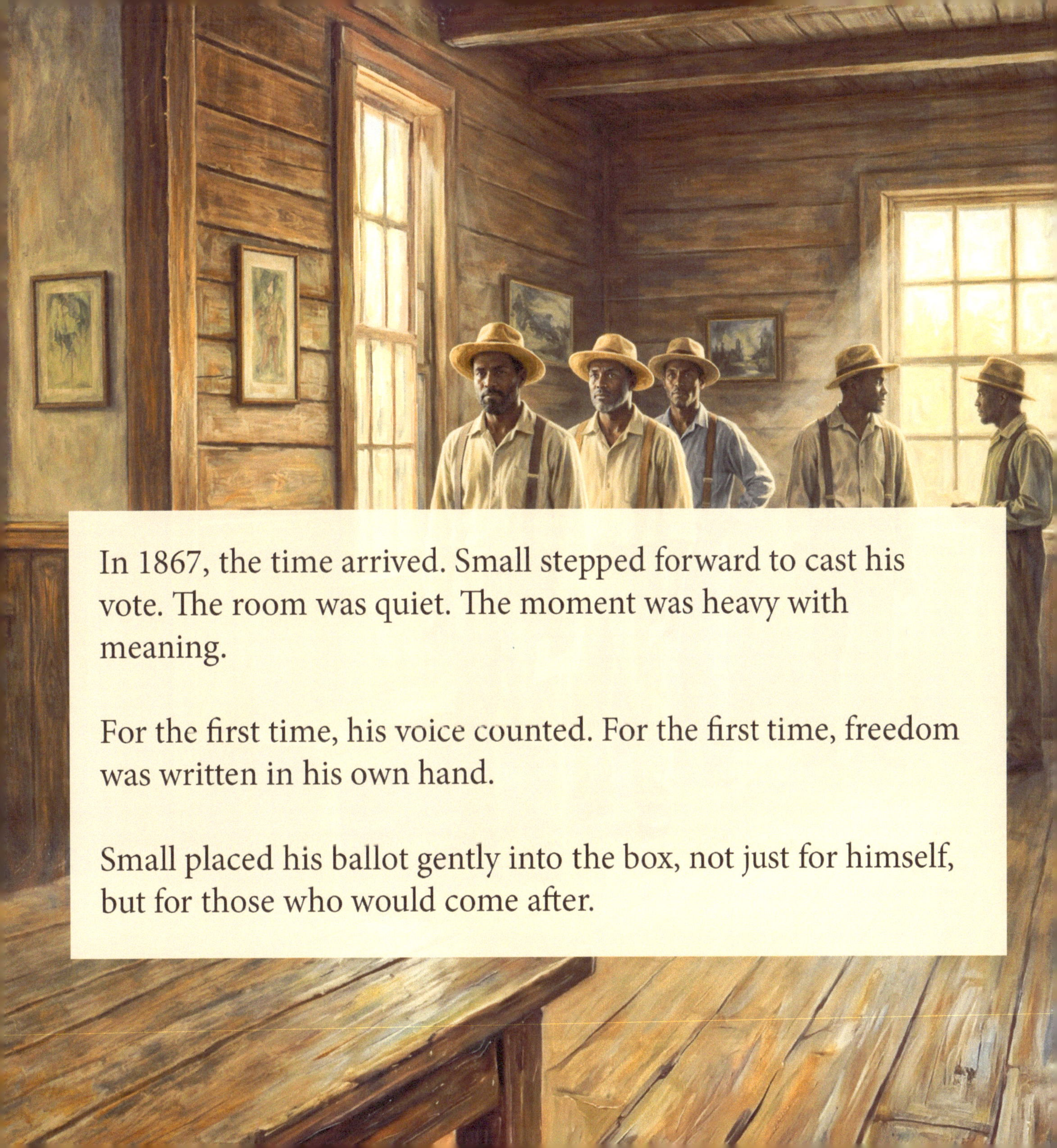

In 1867, the time arrived. Small stepped forward to cast his vote. The room was quiet. The moment was heavy with meaning.

For the first time, his voice counted. For the first time, freedom was written in his own hand.

Small placed his ballot gently into the box, not just for himself, but for those who would come after.

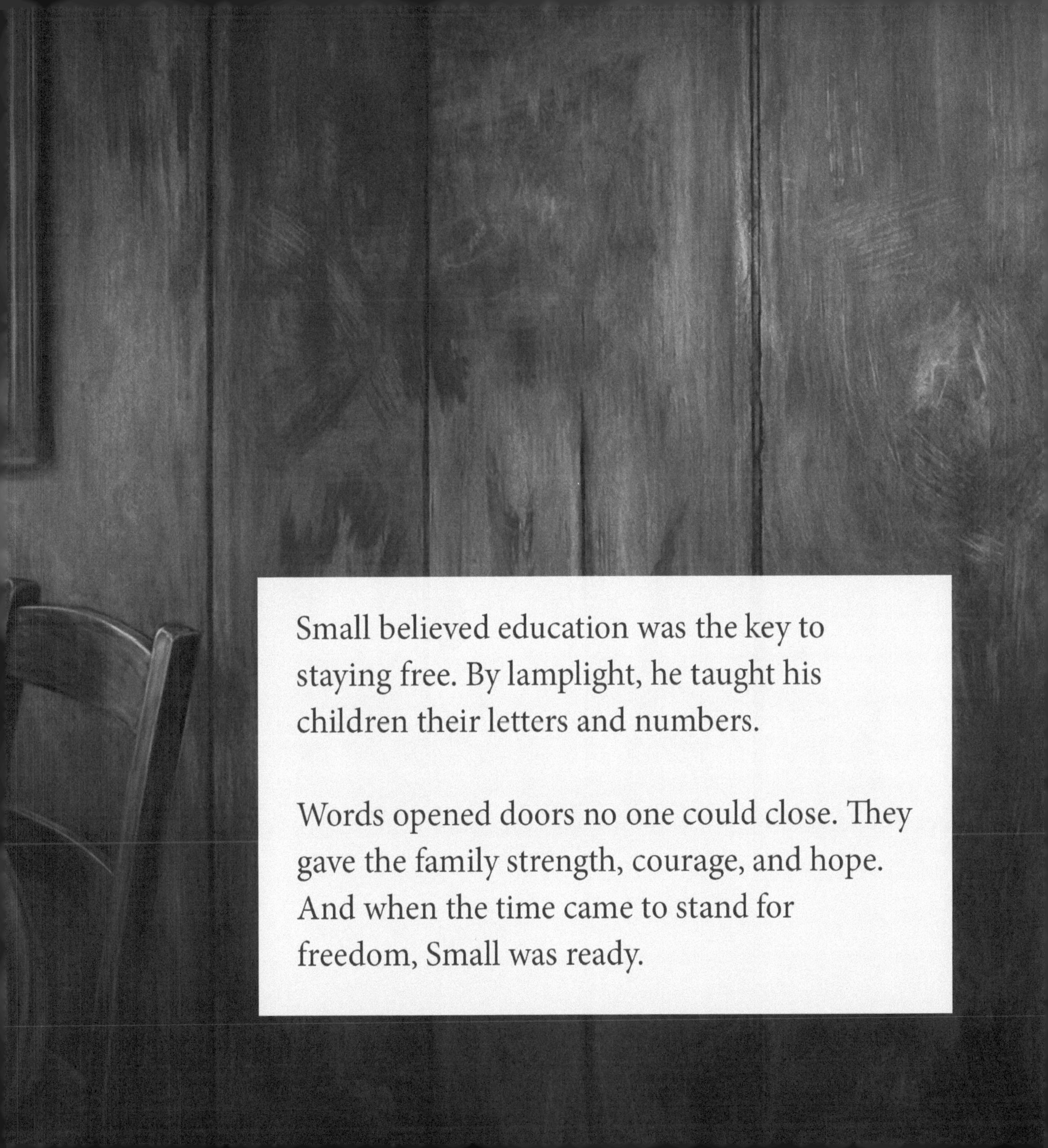

Small believed education was the key to staying free. By lamplight, he taught his children their letters and numbers.

Words opened doors no one could close. They gave the family strength, courage, and hope. And when the time came to stand for freedom, Small was ready.

VOTE

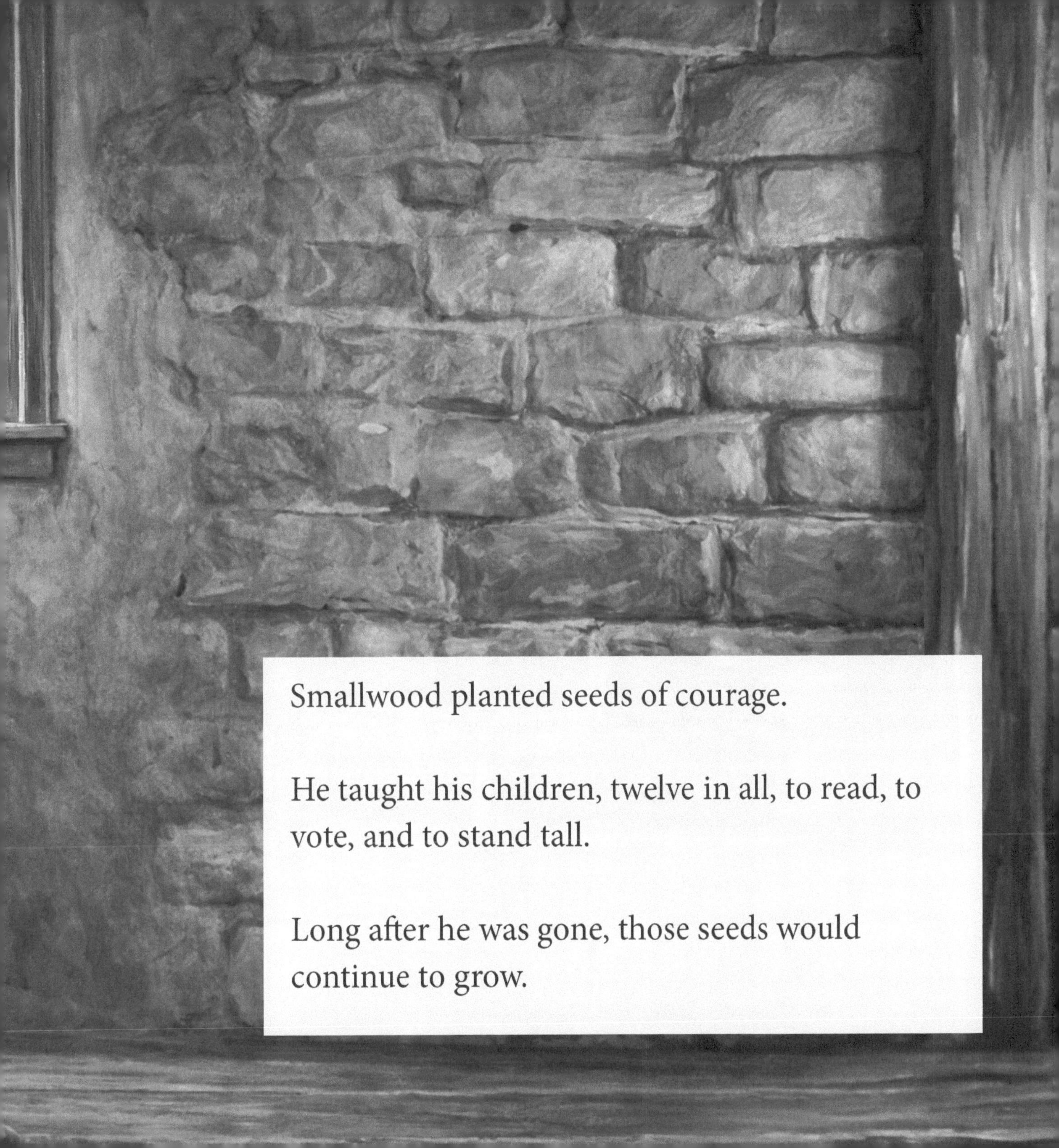

Smallwood planted seeds of courage.

He taught his children, twelve in all, to read, to vote, and to stand tall.

Long after he was gone, those seeds would continue to grow.

Long after he was gone, those seeds kept growing. In his children, and in their children, too.

SUPREME COURT
EQUALITY
VOTE
VOTE
EQUALITY
NOW
FREEDOM
MARCH

Long after Smallwood planted seeds of courage, one of those seeds grew strong and brave.

His great-granddaughter, Evelyn, believed every voice mattered.

She stood before the highest court in the land and helped end the poll tax. So no one would have to pay to vote.

SMALLWOOD ACKISS
CO. E.
23RD U.S.C.T.

Today, the land where Smallwood was once enslaved and later owned is a golf course. On the 15th hole, behind a quiet fence, rests the Smallwood Ackiss Family Cemetery.

Every Memorial Day, our family would return with rakes and flowers. We cleared the weeds and placed bright blossoms.

We told his story. Smallwood's journey was big. His courage still grows.

A Family Legacy of Voting

On February 1, 1864, Smallwood "Small" Ackiss enlisted in the Union Army at Camp Casey, Virginia. He served as a soldier in Company E of the 23rd United States Colored Troops during the Civil War.

When the war ended in 1865, slavery was abolished in the United States. During the years that followed, a time called Reconstruction, newly freed Black men were allowed to vote.

On October 22, 1867, Smallwood Ackiss stood in line in Princess Anne County, Virginia, and voted for the first time.

Nearly one hundred years later, his descendant Evelyn Butts helped challenge laws that made it harder for many people to vote. In 1966, the United States Supreme Court ruled that poll taxes were unconstitutional.

From Smallwood Ackiss to Evelyn Butts, the courage to protect the right to vote continued across generations.

Did You Know?

• During the Civil War, more than 200,000 Black men served as soldiers in the Union Army and Navy.

• Smallwood Ackiss enlisted in the Union Army on February 1, 1864, at Camp Casey, Virginia, and served in Company E of the 23rd United States Colored Troops.

• After the Civil War, Smallwood Ackiss became a landowner in Princess Anne County, Virginia.

• Records show that he voted on October 22, 1867, during the Reconstruction era, one of the first times Black men were allowed to vote.

• The land he once owned is now part of the Cavalier Golf and Yacht Club, where a family cemetery still marks his final resting place.

• Nearly 100 years later, his descendant, Evelyn Butts, helped end poll taxes. In 1966, the United States Supreme Court ruled them unconstitutional.

The Journey Continues

February 1, 1864
Smallwood Ackiss enlists in the Union Army at Camp Casey, Virginia, and serves in Company E of the 23rd United States Colored Troops.

1865
The Civil War ends and slavery is abolished in the United States.

October 22, 1867
Smallwood Ackiss votes for the first time in Princess Anne County, Virginia.

1902
Virginia creates poll taxes that make it harder for many people to vote.

1966
Evelyn Butts helps end poll taxes when the United States Supreme Court rules they are unconstitutional.

Historical Sources

The story of Smallwood "Small" Ackiss is based on historical records and family history preserved by his descendants.

Military records show that Smallwood Ackiss enlisted in the Union Army on February 1, 1864, at Camp Casey, Virginia, and served in Company E of the 23rd United States Colored Troops.

A voter list from Princess Anne County, Virginia, records that Smallwood Ackiss voted on October 22, 1867, during the Reconstruction era.

Local historical accounts document that, after the Civil War, Smallwood Ackiss became a landowner in what is now the Birdneck area of Virginia Beach. That land is today part of the Cavalier Golf and Yacht Club, where a family cemetery still marks the resting place of Smallwood Ackiss and his wife, Charlotte.

Newspaper records report that Smallwood Ackiss died on February 20, 1889, in Princess Anne County, Virginia. The Norfolk Virginian described him as "a prominent and highly respected colored man." (February 21, 1889, p. 1)

Family history and records preserved by his descendants helped guide the telling of this story.

Author's Note

Smallwood "Small" Ackiss was my great-great-grandfather. He was born into slavery in Princess Anne County, Virginia. After the Civil War, he built a life rooted in land, faith, and family.

Family history tells us that he received thirty acres of land after the war, land where he farmed, raised children, and planted more than crops. He planted courage.

Smallwood was among the first Black men in his community to vote after freedom came. At a time when many tried to silence newly freed citizens, he stepped forward.

Generations later, that courage would grow again in our family.

This book is a remembrance and a promise that his story will not be forgotten.

— Charlene Butts Ligon

Notes

Smallwood "Small" Ackiss lived and worked on land in Princess Anne County, Virginia, now part of what is known as the Cavalier Golf and Yacht Club in Virginia Beach.

According to family history, after the Civil War, John Ackiss II granted Smallwood thirty acres of that land. There, Smallwood farmed, raised his family, and began building a life in freedom.

Today, on the fifteenth hole of the golf course, behind a quiet fence, rests the Smallwood Ackiss Family Cemetery. The graves of Smallwood and his wife, Charlotte Ackiss, remain protected and cared for. The site stands as a lasting reminder that history lives beneath our feet.

Records show that Smallwood Ackiss voted during Reconstruction, at a time when Black men were first exercising the right to vote.

Generations later, his great granddaughter, Evelyn Butts, challenged Virginia's poll tax in federal court. In 1966, the United States Supreme Court ruled in Harper v. Virginia State Board of Elections, ending the poll tax nationwide and removing a barrier that had prevented many citizens from voting.

From Reconstruction through the Civil Rights Movement, the fight for the right to vote continued across generations.

Thinking About Courage

Smallwood voted when the right to vote was new and uncertain. Evelyn stood in court when defending that right was difficult and unpopular.

Both believed their voices mattered.

Questions to Consider

- What does courage look like in your community today?
- Why do you think the right to vote is important?
- How can one person make change, even when the problem feels big?
- What "seeds" are you planting for the next generation?

The right to vote has been challenged many times in American history. It has also been protected by ordinary people who chose to act.

Change does not happen all at once.
It grows, one step, one voice, one generation at a time.

For the generations before us,
who stood when it was hard,
and for the generations after us,
who will stand even taller.

SCP
Smallwood Charlotte Press

www.ingramcontent.com/pod-product-compliance
Ingram Content Group UK Ltd.
Pitfield, Milton Keynes, MK11 3LW, UK
UKHW061033310726
14089UKWH00010B/222
9780999383650